Recruiting Game Changers:
Taking Control of Your Recruiting

By Bob Lovell

For Jack.
Dream big and follow your dreams.

Table of Contents

Introduction

The book is called <u>Recruiting Game Changers:</u> <u>Taking Control of Your Recruiting</u> for a reason. Whether you will be recruited or not, whether you will be a scholarship student-athlete or compete in college as a non-scholarship student-athlete, this is the single most important decision you have had to make up to this point in your life. You are making this decision with little or no guidance or help as you try to deal with a tremendous amount of information on the subject.

This book is for two groups of student-athletes. The first group is the elite student-athlete who certainly will become involved in the recruitment process because of their advanced skill level in a particular sport. These are the top players at their respective sports who have already been seen and contacted by NCAA Division I programs. In some cases, these are the student-athletes who have already visited campuses, received scholarship offers, and are in the process of making difficult decisions. The other group, a much larger one indeed, consists of student-athletes who are capable of furthering their athletic careers at the collegiate level, but the level at which they may play is not as clear.

The impetus for this book was countless inquiries from people looking for help in trying to make sense of a process that can be confusing and overwhelming. Even if a parent has played collegiately or coached at various levels, the recruiting world has changed dramatically in a short amount of time. The information in this book is designed to help you formulate a plan to control your own recruitment, because it is hard for parents and student-athletes to be objective about this process, for obvious reasons.

The major objective is to provide student-athletes and parents with the necessary information to aid them in making one of the most important decisions a family will make: where am I going to college? Unless you have been through the experience, it can be confusing, nerve-wrecking, and difficult; you name the adjective and it is appropriate. This is a time of great pressure on the student and his or her parents. You will be asked countless times, "Where are you going to college?" This will also be asked of the parents. My hope is that when you have completed this book, you will have the tools to make important informed decisions, that quite frankly, could be life-altering ones. Where you attend college is one of those major decisions in a young person's life, and too often these decisions are made without necessary information.

Keep in mind, though, that even if you have the necessary information to make this difficult decision, whether or not you will be a scholarship or non-scholarship student-athlete is primarily a decision that will be made by someone else, namely, college coaches. However, the information in this book will help you with those aspects of the process that you can control.

Remember, the more information you have, the better decisions you can make and the better control over your life you will have. Good luck, enjoy the recruiting process as much as you can, and embrace this time in your life as an exciting and rewarding experience.

The Numbers Tell the Story

Talk to any high school student-athlete, regardless of the sport, and they will tell you that they believe they can compete at the college level, and they hope and believe they will receive an athletic scholarship. Talk to any parent of a high school student-athlete, and maybe even parents of junior high school student-athletes, and they believe that their sons or daughters are talented enough to earn an athletic scholarship to compete in college.

Talk to these same student-athletes and many of them even believe they can play professionally after their college careers. Parents and kids dream of playing at the Division I level and eventually playing professionally in their chosen sports. Economic pressures on families fuel these dreams to some degree, but who hasn't dreamed of playing in the "big time"? Many kids and their parents look at sports, and scholarships, as a way to make it financially.

Unfortunately, the statistics reveal that these dreams will be very difficult to achieve. According to the NCAA, about two percent of high school student-athletes are awarded scholarships to compete in college. Add to this total the scholarships that student-athletes receive to play at NAIA and NJCAA schools, and the percentage of students who receive scholarships to compete in college may increase to five percent. A look at this chart from the NCAA will illustrate this point event more:

Athletes	Women's Basketball	Men's Basketball	Baseball	Men's Ice Hockey	Football	Men's Soccer
High School Athletes	452,929	546,335	470,671	36,263	1,071,775	358,935
High School Senior Athletes	129,408	156,096	134,477	10,361	306,221	102,553
NCAA Athletes	15,096	16,571	28,767	3,973	61,252	19,797
NCAA Freshman Positions	4,313	4,735	8,219	1,135	17,501	5,655
NCAA Senior Athletes	3,355	3,682	6,393	883	13,612	4,398
NCAA Senior Athletes Drafted	32	44	600	33	250	75
Percentage: High School To NCAA	3.3%	3%	6.1%	11%	5.7%	5.5%

After graduation or the completion of collegiate athletic careers, an even lower percentage of college student-athletes go on to play professionally than those who received athletic scholarships. Another stat from the NCAA greatly illustrates this point:

Percentage of NCAA student-athletes who become professional athletes:

Men's Basketball - 1.2%
Women's Basketball - 1.0%
Football - 1.8%
Baseball - 9.4%
Men's Ice Hockey - 3.7%
Men's Soccer - 1.7%

These are daunting numbers, but you must be aware of what this all means. Your ability to compete at the college level, and to receive an athletic scholarship will depend on two important factors: skill and academics. You must possess the talent to compete at the highest level, and with the grades and test scores, you will get the opportunity. This book will help you understand what the recruiting process is about, but you still have to be good enough to play, and this is often times not a decision that is up to you or your parents. These decisions are made by college coaches, but you need to understand how decisions are made and what you can do to influence these decisions. This is one of the most important objectives of this book, and I wish you well in the process.

Game Changer #1:
The Recruiting Process – If you want to get
recruited you need to understand the entire process!

In the beginning, an institution of higher education communicates with the student-athlete in an effort to enroll that student-athlete at their institution to become a full-time student and represent a particular athletic team sponsored by that institution. Put a much simpler way, a school wants you to come and play for them. Students at every college and university in the country are recruited: They receive phone calls, e-mails, brochures, catalogues, and other printed information as well as information on the internet. The objective is the same for the school and the prospective student: come to our school to satisfy your academic and social aspirations that will lead to a rewarding life after you graduate.

For our purposes in the athletic world, we will talk specifically about recruitment to play on a particular team at that institution. Coaches on every campus across the country at all levels of competition will engage in the annual ritual that is called recruiting. Every year student-athletes graduate, leave school, choose not to participate, or for a host of other reasons develop the demand that coaches continue to bring in new student-athletes for their team.

Frankly, recruiting never stops, for the coaches or for the schools.

The initial contact in the process normally comes from the collegiate coach, and can come in a variety of forms. E-mails, letters, questionnaires, brochures, or phone calls seem to be the most popular forms of initial contact. The following guidelines should be helpful for you as you try to understand the concept of contacts during the recruiting process.

Printed Materials and E-mails
Men's Basketball and Men's Ice Hockey: June 15 following sophomore year
All other sports: September 1 of junior year
Questionnaires and camp brochures can be sent at any time

Phone Calls
Most sports: July 1 following junior year
Men's Basketball: June 15 following sophomore year
Women's Basketball: April of junior year
Prospects can call coach at any time

Off-Campus Contacts
Most sports: July 1 following junior year

Official Visits
Opening day of classes of senior year

Unofficial Visits
Any time

Obviously, once a student-athlete has been contacted, this can put into place the process we refer to as recruiting. Most of the time, the initial contact from the college coach will be such that it is in the form of a request for information. The request is often times sent to the student-athlete's coach, or can go directly to the student-athlete. The contact letter often consists of a paragraph congratulating the student-athlete on being one of the outstanding players in their area, and of the school's interest in their academic and athletic progress for the upcoming year. The next paragraph gives some basic information about the particular college or university and the specific team. The final few words are for the student-athlete to fill out the requested questionnaire, and wishing them good luck in the future. Please remember that you can receive a questionnaire or camp brochure at any time in the process. The elite player, and the player who only has a chance to play on the collegiate level will mostly receive the same information. Once you receive this initial contact, the student-athlete and his/her family must decide how to respond.

An initial contact, in whatever form, does not mean that you are being recruited by a particular school or schools. An initial contact is just that: a contact. You may just be one of many names on a recruiting list that a particular coach is using to generate a number of student-athletes to recruit. Do not make more of it than what it is: an initial contact. One of the keys is to move from the initial contact to actually being recruited. Understand that recruiting is indeed a numbers game, a game we will delve into later in the book.

Now that you have been contacted, you find yourself in the "potential recruit" category. This is important to know because at the end of the process, you want to move from potential recruit to "signed student-athlete." The immediate question is: What do I do with the initial contact request? If you ignore it, for whatever reason you have in your mind, you may hinder your recruitment. From the college coach's perspective, if you took the time to respond, there is some interest on your part in his school. If you did not respond, would the coach consider that you are not interested and move on to someone who is? That would appear to be fair and accurate. A response is just that; there is no commitment on either side. What harm is there in responding to a contact?

Once you have responded to a contact, you can expect to receive a follow-up letter, e-mail, or phone call from the coach, or staff member, at the aforementioned college of university. This usually comes in the form of "We appreciate your interest. We will closely follow your season, and if you have any questions, do not hesitate to call" type of correspondence. At this point in the process, you are a name on a recruitment list that the coaches are developing for further recruitment. Remember, there are no commitments at this point.

The key for the student-athlete and his/her family is to move from prospective student-athlete to recruited student-athlete. One key distinguishing factor here is that the coaching staff sometimes invites the student-athlete on campus for an official visit, or encouraged the student-athlete and his/her family to make an "unofficial visit" to campus. When you have been asked to come to campus, you can truly consider yourself "being recruited." Look at it this way: prior to being asked on campus, you are an e-mail or phone contact. Coaches may or may not have seen you play in person, at camps, tournaments, or in regular season. You are on a contact list and at that point, nothing else. You certainly may move from the contact list to a recruited athlete, but until you are invited on campus, you are further down the recruitment list.

The "official visit" to an NCAA campus is defined in the following way: Any visit to a college campus by you and your parents paid for by the college. For more information on an official visit, refer to our definition of terms section. Campuses spend money for the official visits, have a limited number of them by rule, and must be judicious with whom they bring to campus. Only those young men and women who have a strong likelihood of being offered a scholarship will be invited for an official visit to campus. If you, as a prospective student-athlete, have not been invited to a campus for an official visit, you may not be someone to whom a college program is interested in extending a scholarship offer.

In addition to a specific number of official visits, many student-athletes will make "unofficial visits" to campuses with whom they have been in contact. An unofficial visit is any visit by you and your parents for which you or your parents pay for the expenses of the trip. Refer to our definition of terms section for more information on unofficial visits. Remember, as long as you or your parents pay, you may take as many unofficial visits at any time you want.

The recruiting process continues after the campus visits and then moves into the offer stage. The scholarship offer stage is obviously only for the schools who participate at the level of competition that allows scholarships, i.e. NCAA Divisions I and II, NAIA Divisions I and II, NJCAA Divisions I and II. NCAA Division III is a need-based aid only level of competition, and extends no scholarship aid based on athletic performance. Schools will extend offers of grant-in-aid to those student-athletes they feel can make contributions athletically, academically, and socially, to their program.

Once an offer has been extended, the responsibility is now on the student-athlete and his/her family and advisors to make a decision. Coaches do this different ways in that some coaches will impose a deadline for the student-athlete to respond, and others will give the student-athlete some latitude with regard to length of time for a response.

With the acceptance of the grant-in-aid offer, the student-athlete has now nearly completed the process. The official signing period varies from sport to sport, and season to season, but the culmination of this process occurs with the student-athlete's and parents' signature of the National Letter of Intent (NLI). While this process may at times seem to move quickly, in many cases it can and does take months to complete. For everyone involved, this process can indeed be a frustrating one, and as you may experience, a complicated one. As we continue through the process, the information I share will hopefully ease your frustrations and make this entire experience more enjoyable to the student-athlete and his/her parents.

Recruiting Process
Evaluation
↓
Contact (Letter, Phone, E-mail)
↓
Response to Contact
↓
Continued Contact and Evaluation
↓
Campus Visits (Official/Unofficial)
↓
Offer of Grant-in-Aid (Scholarship)
↓
Acceptance of Offer of Grant-in-Aid (Verbal Commitment)
↓
Signing of National Letter of Intent

This is an overview of the recruitment process. Generally speaking, this process is the same in many respects for the scholarship and non-scholarship student-athletes.

Takeaways from Game Changer #1

1. Recruiting is literally a never-ending process.

2. Initial contact is just that – an initial contact. Initial contact does not mean you are being

recruited. In the process, you are still a long way from being a recruited student-athlete.

3. If you are contacted, make sure you respond. Why would you want to limit opportunities by not taking time to respond?

4. The recruiting process is not something that happens in a short amount of time. You must be engaged in the process and understand that it will take months or years.

5. The ultimate decision to award grants-in-aids come from the coaches. You are not a scholarship student-athlete until someone offers you a scholarship.

Game Changer #2
If you want to be a scholarship student-athlete, you need to know everything you can about "grants-in-aid."

The best advice for student-athletes is to understand that your ability to qualify for a scholarship, an "initial qualifier," starts with your academic success from your freshman through senior year. What you do, or do not do, in your freshman and sophomore years could greatly impact your ability to qualify for a scholarship immediately after high school.

The responsibility to know and understand initial eligibility requirements rests with you. You cannot wait until you are a senior and expect to make up for your academic deficiencies. You may take yourself out of the opportunity to qualify for a scholarship to a Division I or II school because you did not do well academically as a freshman, sophomore, or junior.

Know these eligibility requirements as well as you can. Ask your counselor and coach for help if you need clarification. Do not wait and pull out the "Nobody told me I had to do that" line. It is your responsibility, not someone else's. Read the following information about Initial Eligibility and take control of your own academic future.

What is a scholarship? It seems to be one of the fundamental questions to ask about this entire process. How do I get one? How much is it worth? How long does it last? What must I do to keep it? These are all valid and important questions about what is referred to as a "grant-in-aid."

A grant-in-aid is a scholarship that can pay for any or all of the following expenses: tuition, room, board, or books.

Necessary fees: on campus fees such as technology, recreation, etc. To be clear, the school is making a considerable financial investment in the student-athlete. To better understand what a scholarship is and how many there are at each school, the following chart will be of invaluable aid:

Sport	NCAA		NAIA	NJCAA
	Mens	Womens		
Baseball	11.7	N/A	12	24
Basketball	13	15	11 (Division I) 6 (Division II)	15
Bowling	N/A	5*	N/A	8
Cross Country	12.6*	18*	5	10 (Combined XC and Half Marathon)
Equestrian	N/A	15*	N/A	N/A
Fencing	4.5*	5*	N/A	N/A
Field Hockey	N/A	12*	N/A	N/A
Football	85 (FBS) 63 (FCS)	N/A	24	85

Sport	NCAA		NAIA	NJCAA
	Mens	Womens		
Golf	4.5	6*	5	8
Gymnastics	6.3*	12 (Division I) 6 (Division II)*	N/A	N/A
Ice Hockey	18 (Division I)* 13.5 (Division II)*	18*	N/A	16
Lacrosse	12.6*	12*	N/A	20
Rifle	3.6*	N/A	N/A	N/A
Rowing	N/A	20*	N/A	N/A
Rugby	N/A	12*	N/A	N/A
Skiing	6.3*	7*	N/A	N/A
Soccer	9.9*	14*	12	18
Softball	N/A	12*	10	24
Squash	N/A	12*	N/A	N/A
Swimming & Diving	9.9*	14*	8	15
Tennis	4.5*	8 (Divison I) 6 (Division II)*	5	9 (3 Full Scholarships, 6 Partial Scholarships)
Track & Field	12.6*	18*	12	20
Volleyball	4.5*	12 (Divison I) 8 (Division II)*	8	14
Water Polo	4.5*	8*	N/A	N/A
Wrestling	9.9*	N/A	8	16

* Denotes Equivalency Sports

When looking at the scholarship limits, it is important to know the difference between a head count sport and an equivalency sport. For example, Men's Basketball is referred to as a "head count sport." In other words, there are thirteen scholarships allowed for Men's Basketball student-athletes to comprise a team. This is not thirteen a year, it is thirteen total for that school. These scholarships are full grants-in-aid, meaning that the financial aid award covers tuition, room, board, books, and necessary fees for that student-athlete for one academic year.

An equivalency sport is much different in the number of scholarships and how they are awarded. For example, women's soccer will have 14 scholarships, but what that really means is that the school can make scholarship awards to student-athletes that total the equivalency of 14 scholarships at that particular school. If, for the sake of example, the soccer squad is comprised of twenty student-athletes, not all will received full grants-in-aid. The notion that all sports give full scholarships is not necessarily accurate. Coaches must be very careful in how they award this limited pool, but there certainly are opportunities for financial aid, albeit partial in many cases in "equivalency sports." One important aspect of scholarships in equivalency sports is the idea of packaging different types of scholarships. For example, you may be able to qualify for an academic scholarship as supplemental aid to the athletic grant-in-aid. Some academic awards do not count toward the team limit which makes you more valuable to the team. However, if you do not have the academic qualifications and have not filled out the FAFSA form, you will not qualify for such an award.

It is also important to know for how long a scholarship is granted. Grants-in-aid are technically awarded on a yearly basis, not to exceed six years. There are circumstances under which the grant-in-aid may be revoked, and there are in fact appeals processes for such revocation. However, you must know that grant-in-aid to NCAA institutions are yearly renewable, i.e. these awards are for one year and can be renewed on an annual basis. There are no guaranteed four year scholarships.

Eligibility Requirements

The most important part of the recruiting process is: will you be eligible to compete at the next level, or will you be sidelined because you didn't fulfill the necessary academic requirements? One important aspect to remember is that you need to begin to focus and concentrate on your academic success as early in the process as possible. Many young men and women arrive at their senior year, have not worked as hard as they should, and find themselves so far behind in fulfillment of initial eligibility requirements that they cannot catch up. The following information will be important for you to know relative to your eligibility concerns.

NCAA Freshman-Eligibility Standards

<u>Core Courses</u>
- NCAA Division I requires 16 core courses as of August 1, 2008. This rule applies to any student first entering any Division I college or university on or after August 1, 2008. See chart below for the breakdown of this 16 core-course requirement.
- NCAA Division II requires 14 core courses. See breakdown of core-course requirements below. Please note, Division II will require 16 core courses beginning August 1, 2013.

<u>Test Scores</u>
- Division I has a sliding scale for test score and grade-point average. The sliding scale for those requirements is shown on page two of this sheet.
- Division II has a minimum SAT score requirement of 820 or an ACT sum score of 68.
- The SAT score used for NCAA purposes includes <u>only</u> the critical reading and math sections. <u>The writing section of the SAT is not used</u>.
- The ACT score used for NCAA purposes is a <u>sum</u> of the four sections of the ACT: English, mathematics, reading and science.
- **All SAT and ACT scores must be reported directly to the NCAA Eligibility Center by the testing agency. Test scores that appear on transcripts will not be used. When registering for the SAT or ACT, use the Eligibility Center code of 9999 to make sure the score is reported to the Eligibility Center.**

Grade-Point Average

- Only core courses are used in the calculation of the grade-point average.
- Be sure to look at your high school's list of NCAA-approved core courses on the Eligibility Center's website to make certain that courses being taken have been approved as core courses. The website is www.eligibilitycenter.org.
- Division I grade-point-average requirements are listed on the next page.
- The Division II grade-point-average requirement is a minimum of 2.000.

Division I 16 Core-Course Rule 16 Core Courses:	Division II 14 Core-Course Rule 14 Core Courses:
4 years of English.	3 years of English.
3 years of mathematics (Algebra I or higher).	2 years of mathematics (Algebra I or higher).
2 years of natural/physical science (1 year of lab if offered by high school).	2 years of natural/physical science (1 year of lab if offered by high school).
1 year of additional English, mathematics or natural/physical science.	2 year of additional English, mathematics or natural/physical science.
2 years of social science.	2 years of social science.
4 years of additional courses (from any area above, foreign language or nondoctrinal religion/philosophy).	3 years of additional courses (from any area above, foreign language or nondoctrinal religion/philosophy)

PLEASE NOTE: Beginning August 1, 2013, students planning to attend an NCAA Division II institution will be required to complete 16 core courses.

Other Important Information

- Division II has no sliding scale. The minimum core grade-point average is 2.000. The minimum SAT score is 820 (verbal and math sections only) and the minimum ACT sum score is 68.
- 14 core courses are currently required for Division II. However, beginning 2010, students will be required to complete 16 core courses.
- 16 core courses are required for Division I.
- The SAT combined score is based on the verbal and math sections only. The writing section will not be used.
- The SAT scores must be reported directly to the Eligibility Center from the testing agency. Scores on transcripts will not be used.
- Students enrolling at an NCAA Division I or II institution for the first time will also complete the amateurism questionnaire through the Eligibility Center website. Students need to request final amateurism certification prior to enrollment.

For more information regarding the rules, please go to www.NCAA.org. Click on "Academics and Athletes" then "Eligibility and Recruiting." Or visit the Eligibility Center website at www.eligibilitycenter.org.

Please call the NCAA Eligibility Center is you have questions: Toll-free number 877-262-1492

NCAA Division I Sliding Scale
Core Grade-Point Average/ Test-Score
New Core GPA / Test Score Index

Core GPA	SAT Verbal and Math ONLY	ACT	Core GPA	SAT Verbal and Math ONLY	ACT
3.550 & above	400	37	2.775	710	58
3.525	410	38	2.75	720	59
3.5	420	39	2.725	730	59
3.475	430	40	2.7	730	60
3.45	440	41	2.675	740-750	61
3.425	450	41	2.65	760	62
3.4	460	42	2.625	770	63
3.375	470	42	2.6	780	64
3.35	480	43	2.575	790	65
3.325	490	44	2.55	800	66
3.3	500	44	2.525	810	67
3.275	510	45	2.5	820	68
3.25	520	46	2.475	830	69
3.225	530	46	2.45	840-850	70
3.2	540	47	2.425	860	70
3.175	550	47	2.4	860	71
3.15	560	48	2.375	870	72
3.125	570	49	2.35	880	73
3.1	580	49	2.325	890	74
3.075	590	50	2.3	900	75
3.05	600	50	2.275	910	76
3.025	610	51	2.25	920	77
3	620	52	2.225	930	78
2.975	630	52	2.2	940	79
2.95	640	53	2.175	950	80
2.925	650	53	2.15	960	80
2.9	660	54	2.125	960	81
2.875	670	55	2.1	970	82
2.85	680	56	2.075	980	83
2.825	690	56	2.05	990	84
2.8	700	57	2.025	1000	85
			2	1010	86

Takeaways from Game Changer #2

1. A grant-in-aid is a financial aid award, a scholarship, from a college or university, that can cover any or all of the following campus expenses:

    a. Tuition

    b. Room

    c. Board

    d. Books

    e. Necessary fees

2. Some sports have full scholarships, and some have partial. The majority of scholarships are not full and you need to be familiar with the opportunities for your sport.

3. Grant-in-aids are for one year only. There are no four-year guaranteed scholarships in NCAA Division I or II.

4. Your must meet Initial Eligibility Requirements to receive financial aid as a freshman at a NCAA Division I or II school. The NAIA also has Initial Eligibility Requirements as well. It is your responsibility to know these requirements well in advance of your senior year of high school.

Game Changer #3

I think I'm good enough, but how do I get recruited to play and receive a scholarship?

This is one of the fundamental questions to be asked and answered in the entire process. We need to ask one basic question in the equation, and that is, are you talented enough, athletically and academically, to be recruited? And if so, at what level of competition? Determining at what level you can compete is at times frustrating, complicated, and often, at the discretion of the college coaches. As we addressed in the previous chapter, you must be academically qualified or your options for recruitment become limited.

Assessing your skill level and matching it up with the right level of competition is never an easy thing. As student-athletes and parents, you are not the most objective sources, and often, you do not fully understand the level of talent at the specific levels of competition. This, in fact, may be one of the most difficult parts of the entire process: at what level can I realistically play? Being able to realistically assess your talent as a player is never easy, but one way to help in this regard is to understand the different levels of competition and how difficult it is to compete at each level.

Levels of competition – NCAA Division I – the highest level of college sports. Grant-in-aid (scholarships) are awarded on a year-to-year basis, and the number of grants depends upon the sport.

Ok, we know what Division I is, but am I good enough to play at that level? How will I know? And will that translate into a scholarship opportunity for me and my family? These are some of the basic and most important questions you want to ask and have answered. Without sounding too callous, you may believe that you are capable of playing at the Division I level, but in many ways, this is a market-driven decision. In other words, you need to be recruited by Division I schools to in fact play at that level, and Division I schools may not share your belief that you have the talent.

One barometer for determining your "value" to the college coaches is the amount of contact you receive from coaches inquiring about your interest in attending their institutions. Look at it this way: if you are receiving interest from Division I schools in your Junior and Senior years of High School, the decision makers believe you may be capable of playing Division I. Always remember that without qualifying academically, you are not going to get the opportunity to compete at the Division I level.

I have always believed that another important way to assess your ability is to listen to the advice of your high school coach. Many coaches have played collegiately, have contacts with coaches at the collegiate level, and may have former players who are currently playing in college, or have done so in the past. To not engage your coach to help assess your talents and potential skill level and level of competition would make absolutely no sense.

Recruiting does not begin when you are a senior, or junior for that matter. More and more, student-athletes are being recruited prior to their junior years in high school, and the process seems to be trending to beginning when student-athletes are as young as eighth or ninth graders. Certainly, this is sport-specific, and what is a trend for football might not necessarily be true of soccer.

This is one of the most difficult parts of the recruiting process to understand. An NCAA Division III football coach described it best by saying "You don't get to choose whether you are a Division I player or not. Someone else will make that decision for you." You, your parents, and coaches may believe you are a Division I player, but that decision is being made by a coach or coaching staff at a college or university program. Another Division III coach put it even more bluntly, "Unfortunately, there are more good players than there are scholarships." This can certainly be said of most sports, not just football. Until a coach makes that scholarship offer, you are still not a "scholarship student-athlete."

One important concept to understand is that recruiting is all about numbers; it is in fact, a "numbers game." In NCAA Division I football, schools are permitted to offer a maximum of twenty-five grants-in-aid per year. Through various methods (camp evaluation, game evaluation, coaches recommendation, scouting services, etc.), Division I football programs will begin each year with a list of 2,000 names, and through the evaluation process, will narrow that down to a number of recruits to be offered scholarships. These schools may make over 100 offers to recruit twenty-five kids, but the average is a 6:1 to 8:1 ratio of offers to accepted scholarships. Remember, the original list was nearly 2,000 names.

In addition to this "numbers game" of converting names to recruits, Division I football coaches will make their decision on players as juniors. Many Division I football programs, especially at the BCS level, will not offer scholarships after July 1st of each year, and seldom will these offers go to a senior in high school. In other words, if you have not been offered a Division I scholarship before your senior year, there is a strong chance you will not get a scholarship to your dream school. You might indeed get a scholarship offer, but it will probably not be from a BCS school.

Much of what has been described in football is also occurring in other sports at the NCAA Division I level. However, at the Division II, III, and NAIA levels, there clearly are opportunities for scholarships offers to high school seniors. Much of this is sport-specific, but the key to remember is to get involved in the process early.

Takeaways from Game Changer #3

1. Be realistic about your ability to compete at the various levels in college athletics.
2. Learn about and become familiar with the levels of competition.
3. You may think you are a Division I player, but that decision will be made by the coaches who run the programs.
4. Recruiting is a "numbers game." A great number of names get converted to recruited student-athletes, who are offered and accept scholarships.
5. Division I scholarship offers are often made to student-athletes during their junior years.

6. Get involved in the process early, and do not wait until your senior year.

Game Changer #4:

How can I make college coaches aware of my talents, or how do I market my skills to receive an athletic scholarship?

To develop a plan to "sell yourself" to prospective colleges and their athletic programs, it is certainly worthwhile to look at how the process works from the perspective of the coaches. You need to know when coaches begin the process, how many players will be in the pipeline, where and when they will see players, how they view highlight videos, how they handle e-mails, and a host of other important parts of the recruiting process. As we discussed in the previous chapter, you do not want to wait until the end of your senior year to think about being recruited. College coaches will tell you recruiting is a year-round, never ending process

With that knowledge, how do you get seen by college coaches? And how do you get a quality look so they can evaluate your talents for a particular sport and a particular level of competition? The most obvious place to start is with your respective team during your high school career. This would seem to be obvious, but in recent years, for certain sports, quite frankly, high school games are not as important for recruiting during the regular season as much as club teams are becoming. College coaches certainly are out at high school games and practices to see and evaluate players. You cannot place a premium on how important it is to play well for your respective high school team.

Club teams and travel teams in many respects are as important as your high school team. As previously mentioned, some sports definitely are trending to situations where there is much more recruitment of student-athletes out of their high school season. This is especially true of volleyball, softball, tennis, soccer, and other sports. Which club or travel team you are a member of is very important, because this team can provide you with one of the key aspects in recruiting: exposure.

Tournaments – for all sports this is a very important part of being seen. To be recruited, you must be committed to playing in tournaments and events when your high school season is completed. AAU basketballs, age group tennis tournaments, soccer tournaments, are all examples of visibility opportunities in which you must be involved. The recruitment process involves so much more than your individual high school team seasons. You could make a compelling argument that what you do out of season in age group tournaments, travel team tournaments, etc., can help you more in the recruiting process than your high school season. You can and will be seen by more coaches in these particular settings because coaches can maximize the number of student-athletes they are able to see at one time. It is imperative that you become involved and engaged in these types of opportunities to be seen and evaluated by college coaches. Work with your high school coach, friends, and anyone who can help you become a part of this process as mentioned earlier. There can and often will be a financial component to these visibility opportunities. You and your family may have to pay for entry fees, equipment, travel (meals, gas, and lodging), camp fees, etc., to become involved in these opportunities. Many look at these expenses as necessary investments in order to receive some sort of scholarship. They are. The more you can be seen, the better your chance for a potential scholarship.

Another great way to gain exposure to college coaches is to attend a sport camp on a college campus. One of the greatest ways to get on the "radar screen" of college coaches is to attend a sport camp at a college where you might have an interest. For example, if you are a soccer player, as a junior high player, or as someone in the ninth or tenth grade, it would be worth your time to attend camps as a way to "be seen."

Obviously, the college coach and his or her staff will be in attendance. Often, student-athletes are encouraged or invited to attend these camps. This is part of the recruitment process, and you should understand the importance of it. Be aware, however, that attendance at camps does in fact have a monetary impact on the families.

The camp experience can be especially important for football players. There are no club or travel team experiences out of season for football players, so attending camps is critical. However, keep in mind that if you are not invited to a college summer football camp, you may not get noticed, so be aware of this important factor. One other important note about camps is to make sure you attend as a sophomore or junior, or attend some of the one day evaluation camps as early in your career as you can to help maximize your exposure.

Another important opportunity for football players is the combine idea. Division I coaches are not currently allowed to attend combines, but Division II, III, and NAIA coaches can. This is an excellent opportunity if you are not currently on the Division I "radar screen."

Takeaways from Game Changer #4

1. Know when the process begins from the college coach's perspective. You do not want to wait

until your senior year in high school to get involved in the process.

2. How do I "get seen" by coaches?

    a. Regular season in high school

    b. Club teams, AAU, age group teams, travel teams

    c. Camps/Combines

3. Depending on the sport, your chance of "being seen" by college coaches can be better in out-of-season competition (not during your high school team's season). Sports such as volleyball, soccer, softball, and baseball, to name a few, are heavily recruited by college coaches during the club or travel team season.

Game Changer #5

If I want more coaches to notice me and in turn help my chances for a scholarship, should I use a recruiting service?

We have discussed at length that part of the process of receiving a scholarship to play intercollegiate athletics is to market yourself and your abilities to compete both academically and athletically. Many parents and student-athletes choose to engage a recruiting service to assist them in receiving an athletic scholarship. It is important for you to identify what recruiting services do, and how they can be involved in the recruitment process so that you can make an informed decision about whether you should pay for their services.

Recruiting services assist the student-athlete and his or her parents by being a conduit between families and college coaches. In other words, recruiting services help compile information, develop a student-athlete profile, and send this information and highlight videos to a database of college coaches. In addition, these services will provide much needed information on the recruiting process, much like information included in this book. Please understand that recruiting services provide a necessary service to families. However, these services come at a price, and that price is often determined by the menu of services provided to families. It is not uncommon for recruiting services to charge upwards of $1,000 - $2,000 per family for their respective programs. This is normally a one-time fee, so if you engage their services when the student-athlete is a sophomore, service is provided for three years for the stated price.

One of the constant themes discussed during this section on how you market yourself has been expenses involved. You must understand that recruiting services are in the business of making money for the services provided. They will mail profiles to hundreds of coaches, help with the highlight video, counsel families on the recruiting process, and basically be a resource for families in this stressful situation. These services have proven successes, and in fact, do provide important information and services to those families who make the decisions to utilize this marketing strategy.

As a family, you need to thoroughly investigate recruiting services, and decide whether you believe in the services and can make the financial commitment. This can be one of the most beneficial decisions you can make in the entire recruitment process.

If, after looking into recruiting services and deciding, for whatever reason, not to hire one, what are your options? At this point in the process, you may want to take control and market yourself, with the help of your family and coaches. One of the selling points for recruitment services is that they contend that your coaches do not have the time or desire to help you contact college coaches, and that your coaches do not have the extensive contact list. That may or may not be true, but to make such a generalization denies the fact that there are very serious and dedicated coaches who work hard to help their student-athletes succeed on the courts and in the fields, and also succeed in recruiting college scholarships. It is imperative that you involve your respective high school coaches as much as you can in the recruiting process.

Certainly, involving your high school coach, as well as other coaches, such as age group or AAU coaches, is a great way to market yourself to college coaches. Your goal is to create as many contacts as possible, and the networks that coaches have are invaluable in this process. As recruiting services do, you want to begin to create your own database of information on colleges and universities and their respective coaches. Focus your database on schools in a geographic area close to your home. For the most part, most student-athletes of all levels tend to gravitate towards schools within a relatively close proximity to their homes, so start your database with schools in your area.

This will be a process that takes time, but you can in fact create your own database. In addition to creating your own database, take the time to research free sites on the internet where you can post your individual profile and highlight video.

Once you have developed the database and found some possible websites to market your academic and athletic skills, you need to develop your own profile and highlight video.

I would encourage you, if in fact you and your family have the financial means, to fully investigate recruiting services and determine if this is the right approach for you. There are a number of very professional, hard-working, and successful recruiting services from which to choose. You must look at this as a "leave no stone unturned" type of situation when looking at what is the best way for you to be recruited.

It is important, also, for you to know how college coaches view the recruiting services and the great amount of information that is sent to the coaches from them. One of the enticing features sited by recruiting services is that they will send your information, your "profile," to an extensive database of college coaches all over the country. These services, do in fact, send quite a bit of information to quite a few coaches. However, what are the college coaches doing with this information?

Many coaches to whom I have talked have mixed feelings about recruiting services. Many Division I coaches said that recruiting services will get your name in front of people, but often it will not translate into scholarship opportunities. Many college coaches believe that the non-scholarship student-athlete benefits more from the recruiting services than the scholarship athlete. Many of these same coaches with whom I've spoken say that they are much more inclined to respond to information sent from the student-athlete and his family, rather than from a recruiting service. They cite the fact that if the student-athlete took the time to submit a profile or highlight video to the college coach directly, that shows a coach this student-athlete has a certain motivation that deserves attention.

It was enlightening to talk to college coaches about recruiting services because the reaction was basically: some coaches read the profiles, some don't, but it seemed that most, if not all, coaches would respond to a profile directly from the athlete himself or herself. The head coach or an assistant were more willing to view those submissions rather than a mass e-mail from an out-of-state address. Many of the coaches of non-scholarship schools said that if a profile came in from out of their geographic area, they would not view it, nor would they view profiles of students who could not qualify academically to be admitted to these coaches' respective schools.

So what is the best way to proceed? As I stated at the beginning of this chapter, if you and your family have the financial means to engage a recruiting service, by all means, do so. But please understand that the reality is that coaches will not view all of the profiles and they are more inclined to view your profile and information if you send it yourself.

Takeaways from Game Changer #5

1. If you have the financial means as a family, working with a recruiting service can be a very useful tool in the recruiting process.
2. Keep in mind most college coaches will respond quicker to information you send rather than information from a third party, i.e. recruiting services

3. Not all coaches view recruiting services in the same way. Some will use them, some won't. Division I coaches may not use them as much as Division III coaches, or use them at all.

Game Changer #6

Your information profile and highlight video, in conjunction with raw game/match footage, can generate interest from coaches.

Part of marketing yourself to college coaches is developing your individual information profile and your highlight video. Part of the advantage to an association with a recruiting service is these tools will be part of their contract with you. This is very important information because in many cases, it might be the first "look" that coaches have of you, and you want to do this well. You can also develop your own information profile and highlight video and post it on a number of free sites such as beRecruited.com.

The information in the information profile is really pretty standard: athletic, academic, and personal information. You will probably want to include a photo, but make sure that you include the following information:

- Name
- Address
- Phone number and best times to call
- E-mail address
- Height
- Weight
- Sport specifics (examples)
  - o 40 yard dash time

- o Bench press
- Vertical jump
- Grade point average (GPA)
- ACT/SAT results (or when you plan to take the test)
- Class rank
- Awards, honors, or other information that showcases your talent
- Schedule of games-in season and out of season (travel, club, AAU)
- Coaches phone number and e-mail address

Send this information to a database of schools that you have compiled that meet your personal criteria. You can make this list as expansive or as limited as you like, but keep in mind you are trying to be seen by as many coaches as you can. Send this profile in conjunction with a cover letter or e-mail, and in that cover letter, thank the coach for taking time to view your profile and highlight video, express your interest in the school, and let them know that you plan to follow up in the next few days.

Highlight videos are among a number of services provided by recruiting services, and these videos serve an important purpose. As stated earlier, one of the keys to your recruitment is to be seen by as many coaches as possible to present your skills and abilities to the scholarship decision makers, and the highlight video can help in that goal. Recruiting services will work with you and your family to put together a first-rate highlight video, and there are also many other companies who will work specifically with you to put together this important tool of your recruitment. Like many other aspects of our lives, you can spend as little or as much time and money as you like to craft a highlight film. It all depends on what your budget may be, and what you want to include in your video.

As with student-athlete profiles sent to college coaches, either by recruiting services or from the student-athlete, the reaction from coaches is somewhat mixed. As you would expect, there are some coaches who will not look at the highlight video because all they will see is the student-athlete doing well and most coaches would prefer to see raw game footage. Coaches want to see actual game situations, not a loop of the same play with the same results on the highlight video. There are also some coaches who will look at the highlight video, but would also like game footage or actual event footage. There is not a "magic formula" for whether to include a highlight video or not, but you may be better served to send, either through a recruiting service or yourself, a combination of highlight video and actual event footage to satisfy both approaches from the coaches.

In putting together the highlight video, remember to make it relatively short, maybe 3-5 minutes in length because coaches are often inundated with videos so it becomes a matter of convenience. Make sure that your name, position, and number appear either in your graphics or in your cover letter. It sounds simple, but make sure you communicate this basic information. This is a highlight video, but you do not want to have the same types of plays or clips where the college coach will basically see the same plays over and over. Try for some variety, different angles or types of situations that will present a different look. Actual event footage should be a little longer than the highlight video, but a simple rule of thumb would be to remember that yours is not the only video being viewed, so present your skills as quickly as you can to spark interest.

If you choose not to engage a recruiting service in your quest to be recruited, many of the coaches with whom I spoke with will definitely view your highlight video and profiles on some of the free internet sites such as beRecruited.com or YouTube.com. As we discussed earlier, some Division I coaches will use these sites, with members of their staffs assigned to watch the videos. However, these free sites where you can post your own video and profile seem to benefit more of the Division II or III student-athletes than the elite, Division I player.

Takeaways from Game Changer #6

1. Coaches would prefer to see actual game or event footage, but some will look at highlight videos.

2. Make sure the highlight video is not too long. Something in the 3-5 minute range.

3. The highlight video can be a part of your recruiting service strategy, or you can put it together yourself and post it on some free internet sites or send it directly to coaches.

Game Changer #7

If it is to be, it is up to me: Developing your recruiting game plan.

This, in fact, may be one of the most important chapters of the book. You need to be in control of your recruitment, and you must be actively engaged and fully understand the process. The best way for me to describe it is how one coach put it when he said, "Kids need to recruit schools in which they have an interest, not the other way around." That may sound naïve in some respects, but there is much truth and wisdom to that coach's statement. You are about to embark on one of the most important four- or five-year experiences in your life, so you need to be in charge of that journey.

The best advice I ever got about coaching was relatively simple: plan for everything, and follow the plan. Putting together your recruiting plan will not be easy, nor simple. However, you must look at this as preparing for a big game or match. You must do your preparation, practice, formulate the game plan, and execute the plan. You do this when you compete. You must do this when it comes to recruiting. Here are some tips for developing your own personal plan.

Freshman and Sophomore Years: At this point in your athletic career, it is imperative to focus on two things: your academic success and continuing to grow and develop athletically. Make certain that you know and understand the initial eligibility requirements and be certain that you are enrolled in the proper curriculum at your high school to meet these requirements. Athletically, you need to do the things the necessary to improve your athletic skills. Play as much as you can, work on skills and athletic development, live in the weight room, and work to secure a spot on the best travel/club teams you can. Remember, there is no substitute for repetitions and you need to play and practice as much as you can.

According to NCAA recruiting regulations, you become a "prospective student-athlete" when you start ninth grade classes. It certainly means that you can never begin to engage in the process too early. By attending a camp at a college or university in which you have interest. Camps are certainly ways in which you can be seen, and make sure coaches know you will be in attendance and that you have an interested in their school. Since you are technically a "prospective student-athlete," you could begin to send your profile information to college coaches at this time in your career. Also, you could begin to schedule unofficial visits to campuses on your "wish list," and make sure the coaches know of your interested in their school. Please be aware that there may not be much interest or response from college coaches, but it will get the process started. Each sport is different, and certainly each level of competition is different in terms of when they begin the recruitment of student-athlete, but you can begin the process at this point in your development as a student-athlete.

Junior Year: From the eligibility standpoint, at the beginning of your junior year you want to make sure that you have registered with the NCAA Eligibility Center. You can do this by logging on to www.eligbilitycenter.org and registering. It is also important that you continue to do as well as you can on your high school course work, and double check to make sure you are taking courses that match your high school's NCAA list of approved courses. Also, at the end of your junior year, you can request that your high school guidance counselor send an official transcript to the Eligibility Center.

During your junior year, you should obviously be working on your athletic skills and performing as well as you can. It is also an important year for you because contacts from colleges will increase. You need to perform well for your high school team, play well in club/travel team play, and make sure you compete in the right tournaments and camps that will give you the most exposure.

Also at this time, you need to begin to formulate a number of schools in which you have an interest. Also, in the ideal situation for you and your family, you will be receiving interest from colleges. Remember, when you receive an e-mail or letter from a college, that is all it is, just a letter or e-mail. You are not being recruited by that school, but at some point in the process, this could in fact become a full-blown recruitment.

It is imperative at this time, if you are not receiving letters or e-mails of interest, to take control of the process and begin to formulate your own list of interest. You want to begin to establish a realistic list of schools in which you would have an interest, and you could start with the following criteria:

- Geographic location – is it close to home so my family can come and see me play on a regular basis?
- Academic programs – does the school offer a degree program in the academic area of your choice?

- Level of competition – certainly most of you will have interest in playing at the Division I level, and you should. You also be realistic about your abilities, but consider this your dream list of schools.
- Campus life – is this a place you want to spend the next four years of your life?

As you are compiling this "dream list" of schools in which you have an interest, make sure you try to keep this list to around 5 to 7 schools. As the process unfolds for you, you will remove some schools from the list, and add others, but this number will work as a good guide for you during the process.

The process to follow is to send your personal information, your profile, and any accompanying statistics or highlight video to the schools on this list. You need to send a schedule or when coaches can see you in club or travel play, or at what camps you will be attending. This is all part of the concept of being seen by as many coaches as possible.

Senior Year: As a senior, you must take the SAT or ACT of often as you feel necessary. The Eligibility Center will use the best scores from each section of the SAT or ACT to determine your best cumulative score. Also as a senior, you need to continue to do as well as you can in your core courses. You need to check to make sure that your high school's courses are on the NCAA list of approved core courses. In your senior year, you also need to request your final amateurism certification. As always, if you have questions, log on to www.eligibilitycenter.org.

Certainly, you will feel a certain pressure during your senior year for a great number of reasons, not the least of which will be the decision on where you will be attending college, and possibly continuing your athletic career. If you can control your recruiting situation, you can lessen the amount of pressure. Try to follow these tips throughout your senior year as you continue the recruiting process:

- Continue to develop the "dream list" of 5-7 schools. Keep in constant contact with the coaches, if nothing more to say that you still have great interest in their particular schools.
- Spend time with your high school, club, or travel team coach to enlist their aid in contacting coaches and supplying information.
- Post your highlight videos on beRecruited.com, iHigh.com, or YouTube.com. Be proactive, send

your profile and highlight video to the coaches. Send follow-up e-mails to the coaches.

- While you want to engage your parents as much as you can in the process, you need to take the lead. Coaches are more inclined to respond to the student-athlete than they are to the parents. You need to be the one making the effort.

At this point in your academic and athletic career, make sure that you have worked as hard as you can in the classroom, on the fields and courts, and in marketing yourself to coaches. There is no guarantee that all of this effort will translate into scholarship opportunities, but not doing this work will certainly not provide opportunities.

Takeaways from Game Changer #7

1. If it is to be, it is up to me – take control of your own recruitment.
2. Make sure you satisfy all of the academic requirements for initial eligibility and you register with the NCAA Eligibility Center.
3. Stay on top of your course work and make sure that your core courses satisfy the NCAA Eligibility requirements.

4. Make sure you take the ACT and/or SAT by your senior year. You can take these exams multiple times.

5. Formulate a "dream list" of 5-7 schools and begin to contact them as early as freshman or sophomore year.

6. By your junior and senior year, contact your list of schools with your profile and highlight video and engage your coaches in the process.

7. Take the initiative of making these contacts yourself!

Game Changer #8

It is my senior year, and I am not being contacted by Division I schools in which I have an interest. What now?

This question may, in fact, contain the essence of this book. After all of your work academically and athletically, your dream of playing at the Division I level may be jeopardized because you are getting little or no response from Division I coaches. This is a very real possibility and it is a situation a great number of student-athletes and their parents have found themselves in.

To review, securing a Division I scholarship is a numbers game, and the opportunities are indeed difficult. You must possess the size, speed, and skill to compete at the Division I level. You may believe you are capable, your parents may believe you are capable, but you must find the coaches and schools who feel you are also capable. If, by the end of your high school season, you have had little or no response or attention from Division I schools, you may need to seriously consider that the coaches who make decisions about who will or will not receive Division I scholarships do not believe that you have the necessary skills for that level. Many athletes and their parents believe if they can just go to one more all-star game, one more combine, one more opportunity of some kind to be seen and evaluated, the Division I offer will be forthcoming. In most cases, this does not happen. There are, however, exceptions to these circumstances, but most of the time you will not benefit from the "one more chance" situation for the Division I offer.

If you are in this situation, have sent your profiles and highlight videos, contacted the coaches, had your coach call on your behalf and the Division I offer is not there, this does not mean scholarship opportunities have evaporated. NCAA Division II, NAIA Divisions I and II, NCJAA schools all have varying levels of athletic grants-in-aid (scholarships) available. One of the most important things you need to do now is to acknowledge that you may not, in fact, play at the Division I level. Dreams die hard as we all know, and I always encourage people to aim high and follow their dreams. You may still have the opportunity to become a "preferred walk-on" at a Division I program, and you must consider this option. Please keep in mind that there is no guarantee there will be a scholarship if you begin the program as a "walk-on." Often time the student-athletes hear the words "chance for a scholarship" and we are all aware of times where a "walk-on" has actually received a scholarship. However, the percentages are not in your favor to receive a scholarship if you accept the "walk-on" option.

If the Division I opportunity is not there for you, your next scholarship opportunities may be at the Division II, NAIA, and NJCAA levels. You now must go back to the basics of marketing yourself to coaches at those levels. You must contact, or in some cases, re-contact coaches and find out about their interest in you. You must also revise your wish list of schools to include those who are not at the Division I level, but again, within the 5-7 range of schools in which you have interest. You need to send the profiles and highlight videos, and make personal contact with coaches via e-mail or by phone, if possible. Also, it would be of great benefit to have your high school, club or travel coach contact the college coaches, if they can, to talk about you and the value you could bring to a college program.

Let's assume that your season has concluded. Opportunities have not been forthcoming, and you are understandably concerned. This is also a time that, if you have not already done so, and have the financial means, you might want to contact a recruiting service and enlist their services to maximize your opportunities.

Earlier in the book we discussed the concept of scholarship player vs. non-scholarship player, and that in many ways is often where the recruiting process ends – the determination of who will be awarded grants-in-aid and who won't. If you reach your senior year, and your season has ended and there are no scholarship opportunities afforded you, the process has evolved and you must now make some decisions. Many young men and women decide that since they did not get a scholarship, they will attend the institution of their choice and not play at the college level. These decisions are personal ones, and obviously very difficult to make. I strongly urge student-athletes and their families not to take the approach of "Well, I didn't get a scholarship, so I will just go to school." When you take this approach, you are saying that the only reason you competed or wanted to compete was because you wanted a scholarship. There are numerous opportunities to get a great education and participate in intercollegiate athletics at non-scholarship schools. I strongly believe you do yourself a disservice by not considering non-scholarship opportunities that may be available to you.

Takeaways from Game Changer #8

1. After your senior season has completed, and you have no scholarship offers, renew your self-marketing strategy with much greater urgency.

2. Make weekly contact with your list of 5-7 schools. Send personal e-mails, profiles, and highlight videos.

3. Enlist the aid of your coaches in contacting schools.

4. Bring yourself and your family to the realization that Division I opportunities are not available, and you need to re-evaluate your options.

5. Contact Division II, NAIA, and NJCAA schools and market yourself to these institutions.

6. If you have the financial means, contact a recruiting service that can help you maximize your exposure.

Game Changer #9

Scholarship opportunities were not available at the conclusion of your senior season, but a non-scholarship school could be a great opportunity to get a great education and continue to compete.

This may be the "You can't always get what you want, but if you try sometimes, you just might find, you get what you need" scenario so ably stated by The Rolling Stones. Your Division I aspirations have not come to fruition, no scholarship offers were coming your way from NAIA or Division II schools, so now what do you do? This puts you in the non-scholarship student-athlete situation we have discussed earlier in the book. NCAA Division III athletics can be a tremendously rewarding experience, both on and off the fields and courts, but many people do not fully understand what the Division III level is all about and how you have to approach it.

NCAA Division III athletics do not offer grants-in-aid based on athletic participation at member institutions. But Division III schools will offer grants for academics and other institutional awards to those student-athletes who qualify academically. Another source of aid for the prospective student-athlete is in the form of institutional aid for which the family qualifies based on the submission of the FAFSA (Free Application for Federal Student Aid) form. Please note and remember the FAFSA is the first step in getting financial aid, and you must submit this form by March 10 to be eligible for financial aid at the state level.

One of the most common mistakes families make is failing to submit the FAFSA because they feel like as a family they may not qualify for financial aid. Most financial aid experts urge families to file the FAFSA regardless of whether you feel you will qualify or not. Make sure you file and make sure that you do it before the deadline. If you have questions about this extremely important part of the process, contact a financial aid counselor at local colleges or call 1-800-433-3243. Understanding the financial aid process is a first step in fully understanding Division III athletics.

Many people mistakenly underestimate and do not appreciate the skill level and competitiveness at the Division III level. More student-athletes compete at the Division III than at Division I, and in many cases, find the experience to be rewarding academically and athletically. Certainly, the attitude at the Division III level is to participate because you enjoy your sport, and unlike the Division I level where most of your time is controlled, you can have an enriched educational experience off the fields and courts!

The difference between the campus experience at the scholarship level as opposed to the experience at the non-scholarship situation can be what each individual makes it. However, fundamentally, you have more time to devote to academics and activities outside of the classroom at the Division III level. Your motivations are somewhat different at the scholarship schools. Quite frankly, when you compete as a scholarship student-athlete, you do not control your time. You have very little, if any, say in how you will use your time out of competition or practice, but the reward is the scholarship and the opportunity to compete at the highest level.

Division III coaches will often times begin their recruiting process in the spring, looking at the senior class of the upcoming year. They will try to develop as expansive a list as possible at that point, and try to narrow down the number of prospects as the season unfolds. Realistically, coaches know that student-athletes are not really thinking about Division III athletics until they are seniors or late in their junior years. To simplify, Division III coaches recruit next year's class after May. They will cast a big net to convert their numbers of prospects into a smaller number of committed student-athletes. These Division III coaches will approach the recruiting process in the same manner as Division I by going to games, camps, subscribing to recruiting services, viewing videos, talking to coaches and all of the other ways we have discussed in the evaluation process. The Division III process is lengthier before decisions are made because schools, parents, and student-athletes normally wait until the spring before financial aid awards are presented. However, early in the process, coaches make decisions on prospects based primarily on academic performance. If you express an interest in a Division III program, coaches will look first at your academic record to see if you, in fact, can be admitted and if you are interested in an academic discipline offered by that particular college or university. Obviously, doing well academically, as we have discussed, is an important part of the process relative to Division III athletics.

Participating at the Division III level can be rewarding as we have discussed but you must make sure you do the following things and diligently follow-up with coaches:

- File the FAFSA form prior to March 10.
- Apply for admission as early as you can to schools on your list.

- Contact the Division III coach personally via e-mail, phone, or letter.
- Send profile, highlight video, raw footage of games or matches to coaches.
- Finish your senior year strongly from an academic standpoint.
- Come to terms mentally and emotionally that you may not be a scholarship student-athlete, but there could be great opportunities to participate and receive an outstanding educational experience.

Takeaways from Game Changer #9

1. Non-scholarship (Division III) schools do not give athletic scholarships. You can receive grants from the institutions, but not for the express purpose of competing on a sports team.
2. Realize that there are great opportunities at the non-scholarship level, and embrace that concept.
3. File the FAFSA on time, before March 10.
4. Understand that the Division III experience can be an exciting one, one in which you can control more of your time in and out of season.
5. Continue to follow the suggestions to market yourself to coaches at the non-scholarship level, i.e. e-mail, profiles, highlight videos.

6. If you have questions about financial aid, contact schools financial aid staff in which you have an interest.

Game Changer #10

Junior Colleges have some advantages and disadvantages for your academic and athletic needs.

To this point, our discussions on the recruiting process have focused on opportunities at four year institutions. The Junior College level does, in fact, offer student-athletes and their families another alternative in the process, as there are scholarships opportunities available in a great number of sports. The Junior College level is one that is often not fully understood or appreciated for the experience a student-athlete can achieve academically and athletically. It is not, as many believe, a level where you go because you do not have the academic record to be an initial qualifier at an NCAA Division I or II school. Certainly there are a great number of student-athletes who fit that profile who go to a Junior College, but not all student-athletes make that move.

There are many advantages to attending a Junior College to continue your athletic and academic career. You can, in fact, improve your academic skills and improve your grades so that you could qualify for grants-in-aid at NCAA Division I and II schools. You will also play a great number of games and have longer season with more competition that will hopefully improve your athletic abilities. Some student-athletes who are physically late developers realize great benefits from attending Junior College because it allows them to grow physically and the student-athlete can refine his or her athletic skills.

The clear disadvantage to attending a Junior College is that you will have to go through the recruiting process one more time. That, in fact, may be an advantage in that you will or should understand the process much better, but you will still have to make a decision on where you want to continue your education. In addition, you will be attending at least two schools during your career and will only be at these schools for a limited amount of time.

The recruiting process at the Junior College level is different than what we have previously discussed. There are scholarship opportunities at the Junior College level, and as in the NCAA, there are different levels of competition and different scholarship opportunities. If your primary motivation is to receive a scholarship, and possibly the opportunity to continue at an NCAA Division I or II schools, those opportunities exist at the Junior College level. Coaches at the Junior College level will be engaged in contacting student-athletes prior to and during their high school seasons, but often will begin contact during the student-athletes' senior year. Junior College coaches realize, like most student-athletes and their parents, that kids will aspire to receive the Division I offer, so Junior College coaches often wait until these decisions have been made.

Looking at the Junior College level as a last resort-type of decision would not be fair or accurate. Because of the process, often student-athletes will try to secure a scholarship before they commit to a Junior College. That seems to be standard operating procedure for the process. If you know you will not be an initial-eligibility qualifier, you might want to speed up the process and engage Junior Colleges as soon as you can. However, Junior College commitments come later in the process.

Also important in the process is to understand all of the personal marketing and exposure ideas we have previously discussed. You must make Junior Colleges aware of you academic and athletic skills and you must include them on your contact list. Send your profile, highlight video, and other pertinent information. The process is reasonably the same for the Junior College coaches.

Takeaways from Game Changer #10

1. If your desire to receive a scholarship did not happen at the NCAA Division I level, there are

opportunities at Junior Colleges in a great number of sports.

2. You can improve your academic and athletic skills at the Junior College level.

3. You can qualify and if talented enough, receive a scholarship once you leave Junior College.

4. There are advantages and disadvantages to attending a Junior College. One advantage is you can develop as a player. One disadvantage is you will have to go through the recruitment process once again.

Game Changer #11

I have been through the process, but now I need to make a decision. What should I consider when making one of the most important decisions of my life?

This is what the whole process is about: making a decision. When you begin to put some perspective on this, many people meet their future spouses at college. A great number of people meet and forge their strongest friendships with people from their college days. There are many more examples of how important this collegiate experience can be.

Every piece of information to this point has been to bring you to making your decision. Frankly, in many respects, this game changer could easily come at the beginning of the book because it sets down some parameters and guidelines for a decision that you should think about from the beginning.

During most of my coaching career, I would tell recruits to take athletics out of the equation, and make a decision about where the student-athlete would be comfortable with the campus, challenged academically, and engaged in a major that provided career opportunities, and an environment where their academic and social needs would be nurtured. You are having the same reaction that student-athletes and their parents had when I had these conversations: that all sounds great but we are going to make a decision primarily based on money and playing time. As much as I would like it to not be this way, too many decisions are based on those factors.

When you begin the recruiting process, you should always strive to find a school where you will feel comfortable. You will be there for four or five years. You absolutely need to find a place where you feel comfortable with the people and the environment. One college coach described the decision process well when he said that you should not let it drive you, you should drive it. Your college choice should not be driven by who is interested in you; rather, it should be about whom interests you.

This all sounds great, but the reality of the recruiting process is that you will more than likely be driven by who is recruiting you, if in fact you have the opportunity to receive a scholarship. Whatever your motivation or your philosophy of the process, there are still a number of important factors to consider as you make this extremely important decision. The following points should be of great value as you look to make a choice:

I.   The University

a. Does the university offer the curriculum which will enable me to enter the profession I desire after graduation?

b. What is the placement record for graduates of the curriculum I wish to take?

c. What is the university's overall academic rating with regard to similar institutions?

d. Are my high school grades adequate for admission to the universities in the curriculum I desire?

e. What percentage of athletes in my sport receive a degree from the university and do they receive it in a four, five or six year period?

f. Is the university well publicized in the part of the country where I plan to make a living in the future, and is the university well publicized where I graduated from high school?

g. Can I afford to travel home during vacation periods and can my parents and girlfriend/boyfriend afford to travel to the university to see me play as often as they wish?

h. Is there an opportunity for post-season play, or is the conference dominated year in and year out by one or two teams? Is this an independent that has difficulty getting a post season bid?

i. Does the schedule demand excellence of play and is it attractive by providing interesting experiences in travel as well as play?

j. Do I have friends at the university and what do they think of the academic as well as the athletic program?

k. Do I like the community and surrounding area where the school is located and does it offer a variety of experiences for me?

II. The coaching staff at the university

a. Do I like the head coach, the assistant coaches, and all others I have met who are directly connected with the team and the university?

b. How long has the head coach been at the university and does it appear he/she will be there throughout my four year stay?

c. What do the current players think of the coach and the coaching staff? Evaluate their answers carefully as the current players issues and situations may not affect you.

d. Does the coach have basically the same offensive and defensive philosophy that my high school coach has? Will I either fit in well into the style of play or the university or can I easily adjust to a different system of play?

e. Are the coaches sincere and honest to the best of my knowledge? Do they demonstrate concern for me as a person as well as a player? Do they seem interested in my health and academic progress? HAVE THEY OFFERED ME AN ATHLETIC SCHOLARSHIP?

III. The position

a. Will I play as a freshman and how much? If not, am I willing to accept that? What is the past history of playing freshman?

b. As a general practice, are transfer and junior college players recruited?

c. Who is graduating from the current team and what position do they play?

d. What are my chances of playing professionally as a result of my playing experience at this university?

IV. Personal considerations

a. How much does the school cost over and above the scholarship?

b. Is there a possibility of summer employment either near campus or at home as a result of my affiliation with the university?

c. Who pays for summer school if attendance is necessary?

d. Should I fill out the questionnaire and how do I narrow the number of schools to visit? Any school ruled our because of preconceived criteria, not necessarily because of first impression?

e. Deep down inside, am I convinced that I can compete in this league, at this level of competition, and make a valuable contribution to the future success of the program?

f. What is my high school coach's opinion of the universities I am considering? Can he provide insight on the style of play, returning players and the relationship of the college coach with his previous players?

KEY: The key here is that the player makes the final decision. If someone tries to make the decision for the player, he will have a built in excuse if and when things do not go as he thinks they should. It is like getting married – a lot of people can express opinions, but, in the last analysis, it is up to the individual to make the decision. There is no way to be 100% sure, but, if it seems natural and the right thing to do, then it probably is.

You should also take an honest and ethical approach to making this decision. The following points should be of help to you as you work through the process.

I. First, ask yourself these questions.

a. What are my academic capabilities?

i. What is my rank in class?

ii. What are my standardized test scores?

iii. What is my grade point average?

b. What are my athletic capabilities?

i. Height – Am I tall enough?

       ii. Weight – Do I weigh enough?

      iii. Speed – If I am not big, am I very fast?

      iv. Physical skills

   c. For what profession do I want to prepare?

   d. What are my financial resources?

   e. Do I want to "go away" to school or do I want to remain close to home?

II.   The Recruiting Game

   a. The athlete's approach to the recruiters

      i. I will approach the possible opportunity of going to college as a privilege and an honor. I will become dedicated to the principle that I will make a major contribution to the university and not take the too common attitude, "What is in it for me?"

      ii. How many colleges and universities am I honestly interested in visiting?

      iii. If I expect recruiters to be honest with me, <u>I should be honest with them!</u>

  iv. Visits to college campuses should not interfere with my high school academic or athletic activities. Trips should be made on weekends or during vacation periods.

b. What should be the athlete's expectations of the recruiter?

  i. Honesty with the athlete and his parents

  ii. No promises of aid beyond that allowed by the rules of the college or university, the conference and the sanctioning body – i.e., NCAA, NAIA, NJCAA

  iii. The coach and his staff follow whatever rules you and your family, your coach, and your high school establish for their contact with you.

  iv. The coach and his staff familiarize themselves with your academic qualifications as well as your athletic skills.

v. Campus visits are scheduled that take into account your academic and athletic schedule.

vi. All university, conference and sanctioning body standards for campus visits are followed.

vii. All scholarship offers are in writing and contain amount, terms and duration.

At this point, you can easily say that you have been given quite a lot of information to digest. You do not want to fall victim to the "paralysis through analysis" situation because of all the information. However, this needs to be the decision of the student-athlete in consultation with parents, coaches, and others. But it must finally be the decision of the student-athlete. He or she will be the one who will be living the decision, and it needs to be theirs. For a number of reasons, this decision must be made in this manner.

Many will tell you to follow your heart; you will know what is right; and a host of other clichés. When you make this decision, make sure you have considered all of the information, the people involved, and the other important factors, and make your decision on your own set of criteria. Make sure you take control of your own recruitment.

Takeaways from Game Changer #11

1. This could be one of the most important decisions of your life, so take time to carefully deliberate and make a decision.
2. Try to find a place where you feel comfortable academically and athletically.
3. Do not make a decision based only on money.
4. Be ethical and honest in the process.
5. Student-athletes: it is your decision to make. Consult mom and dad, but make sure you make the decision.

Game Changer #12

What is a Letter of Intent and what does it mean to "sign" with a school?

The recruiting process ends with the signing of a National Letter of Intent (NLI). The NLI program is a voluntary one with regard to the institutions and the student-athletes. The NCAA Eligibility Center manages the daily operations of the NLI program, while the Collegiate Commissioners Association (CCA) provides governance oversight.

By signing a National Letter of Intent, the student-athlete agrees to attend the designated institution for one academic year. The particular school agrees to provide athletic-related financial aid for one academic year, provided the student-athlete is admitted to the school and is eligible to receive financial aid under NCAA rules. Another important element of the NLI is that once a student-athlete has signed the NLI, institutions that participate in the NLI program must end their recruiting of the student-athlete.

The NLI program deals with initial enrollment at four year institutions for student-athletes who are first time enrollees. It also covers student-athletes who are graduating from a two-year college. When you sign an

NLI, you must receive a written offer of athletic financial aid that lists the teams and conditions plus the amount and duration of the aid award.

If you do not attend the institution at which you signed the NLI for one full year and enroll at another institution that participates in the NLI program, you may not compete in intercollegiate athletics for one academic year. Also, you will be charged with the loss of one season of eligibility.

If you feel the need to be released from your NLI obligation, there is an appeals process you can initiate. This appeals process can be initiated if the original signing institution denies your request for a release. You will need the release request form, and the NLI Policy and Review Committee is authorized to review, issue interpretations, settle disputes, and consider petitions for release from provision of the NLI.

The NLI becomes null and void if you are denied admission by the signing school. In addition, you must meet the institutions requirements for financial aid and the NCAA requirements for financial aid. You also must provide information to the NCAA Eligibility Center for an initial-eligibility decision.

You must understand that you have signed the NLI

with an institution and not a specific coach, and if that coach leaves the institution, you are still bound by the NLI. You may request a release from your NLI, and you will have to go through the aforementioned process. The school may not grant your release, but you do have an appeals process. There are some student-athletes who sign institutional agreements of financial aid and are not bound by the NLI. If there is speculation that a coach may not return, this allows the student-athlete to not be bound by the NLI restrictions, and the recruiting process could continue. This situation does not happen very often because schools will obviously want your signature on the NLI and your commitment to the school.

The signing of the National Letter of Intent should be a momentous and joyous occurrence, a culmination of years of hard work, and dedication. It also signifies the completion of the recruiting process, a process that can and will take many turns and twists until completion. Before the signing of the NLI, make sure you fully understand the provisions, and what your responsibilities are, so that you can fully enjoy and appreciate the final act of your recruitment.

Takeaways from Game Changer #12

1. The recruiting process is completed with your

signature on a National Letter of Intent.

2. By signing an NLI, you agree to attend the institution for at least one year, and in return will receive athletic financial aid.

3. If you do not attend the school with whom you signed, and do not receive a release, you will not be allowed to compete for one year and be charged with a season of competition.

4. If the coach who recruited you leaves the school, you may request a release from the NLI, and if the school does not allow it, you can appeal to the NLI.

Recruiting Definitions

Contact

A contact occurs any time a coach has any face-to-face contact with you or your parents off the college's campus and says more than hello. A contact also occurs if a coach has any contact with you or your parents at your high school or any location where you are competing or practicing.

Contact Period

During this time, a college coach may have in-person contact with you and/or your parents on or off the college's campus. The coach may also watch you play or visit your high school. You and your parents may visit a college campus and the coach may write and telephone you during this period.

Dead Period

The college coach may not have any in-person contact with you or your parents at any time in the dead period. The coach may write and telephone you or your parents during this time.

Evaluation

An evaluation is an activity by a coach to analyze your academic or athletics ability. This would include visiting your high school or watching you practice or compete.

Evaluation Period

The college coach may watch you play or visit your high school, but cannot have any in-person conversations with you or your parents off the college's campus. You and your parents can visit a college campus during this period. A coach may write and telephone you or your parents during this time.

Official Visit
Any visit to a college campus by you and your parents paid for by the college. The college may pay the following expenses:
• Your transportation to and from the college;
• Room and meals (three per day) while you are visiting the college; and
• Reasonable entertainment expenses, including three complimentary admissions to a home athletics contest.

Before a college may invite you on an official visit, you will have to provide the college with a copy of your high school transcript (Division I only) and SAT, ACT or PLAN score and register with the NCAA Eligibility Center.

Prospective Student-Athlete
You become a "prospective student-athlete" when:
• You start ninth-grade classes; or
• Before your ninth-grade year, a college gives you, your relatives or your friends any financial aid or other benefits that the college does not provide to students generally.

Quiet Period
The college coach may not have any in-person contact with you or your parents off the college's campus. The coach may not watch you play or visit your high school during this period. You and your parents may visit a college campus during this time. A coach may write or telephone you or your parents during this time.

Unofficial Visit
Any visit by you and your parents to a college campus paid for by you or your parents. The only expense you may receive from the college is three complimentary admissions

to a home athletics contest. You may make as many unofficial visits as you like and may take those visits at any time. The only time you cannot talk with a coach during an unofficial visit is during a dead period.

Verbal Commitment

This phrase is used to describe a college-bound student-athlete's commitment to a school before he or she signs (or is able to sign) a National Letter of Intent. A college-bound student-athlete can announce a verbal commitment at any time. While verbal commitments have become very popular for both college-bound student-athletes and coaches, this "commitment" is NOT binding for either the college-bound student-athlete or the school. Only the signing of the National Letter of Intent accompanied by a financial aid agreement is binding on both parties.

SOURCE: NCAA.org

Reference Information

Keep this page handy as it will help you find some of the necessary information for your recruiting questions.

www.recruitinggamechangers.com - Stay in touch for updates of important information.

www.NCAA.org - This should be bookmarked as it will answer a great number of your questions.

www.NAIA.org - This should be bookmarked as well. Scholarship opportunities are available.

www.NJCAA.org - Great information from the junior college level.

www.eligibilitycenter.org - At the beginning of your junior year, make sure you are registered with the NCAA Eligibility Center.

www.fafsa.ed.gov - Must use this site to file for financial aid.

www.beRecruited.com - Free site for recruiting. Many coaches visit this site on a regular basis.

www.iHigh.com - Free recruiting site.

www.YouTube.com - We are all familiar with this site, and many coaches will visit and look at players.

www.facebook.com - Have your own account and make coaches aware of your highlight video and profile.

About the Author

Bob Lovell has been involved in intercollegiate athletics as a coach and administrator for nearly thirty years and has been in sports media for the past sixteen years. Lovell was the basketball coach at Franklin College and IUPUI, and served as the IUPUI Athletic Director for ten years. Lovell also spent seven years at the Horizon League as the Senior Associate Commissioner for External Affairs and Director of Basketball Operations. For the past sixteen years, he has hosted *Indiana Sports Talk* on Network Indiana and will be inducted into the Indiana Sportswriters and Sportscasters Hall of Fame in April 2011. Lovell and his wife Penny reside in Franklin, Indiana and are the parents of one daughter, Stephanie Kleinrichert (Gary), and one grandson, Jackson Lovell Wheeler.

Acknowledgement

A book of this kind is not possible without the support and encouragement of a number of people. Thanks, first, to my wife Penny for her patience and gentle reminders to complete this book. My thanks to my daughter Stephanie Kleinrichert and her husband Gary for their insights and encouragements, Heath Shanahan for his tireless efforts, Mo Wildey for his guidance and vision, Stephanie Jarvis for her great legal and compliance advice, Sarah Miller for the outstanding cover design, Ashley Reed for her photography work, Gary Thoe for his help through the publishing maze and his constant support, Dana Thomas for her support, Daniel Comiskey for his great edits and advice, my colleagues at Emmis Communications for their understanding and support, Eric Wunnenberg for his great insights, and coaches Bill Lynch, Bill Fenlon, Rodney Watson, Kerry Prather, Mike Leonard, Dale Carlson, Jim Shaw, Marty Simmons and Shannon Griffith for their time, thoughts, and support. Thank you all for your help and support.